Emotions

Emotions
"Scattered Expressions"

Written by
Juanita Edwards

Emotions

Emotions "Scattered Expressions"
Written by Juanita Edwards

© Copyright Emotions "Scattered Expressions"

All Rights Reserved.

No part of this book may be reproduced, scanned, or transmitted in any forms, digital, audio or printed, without the expressed written consent of the author.

Pa-Pro-Vi Publishing: www.paprovipublishing.com

ISBN# 978-1-959667-83-4

Emotions

Table of Contents

Dedication 6
Emotions 7
Where Did The Love Go? 12
In My Feelings 15
Home Alone 18
Much Too Busy For Me 20
In Memory Of 22
Notice Me 24
Where Are You? 26
Why Me? 28
Ideal Husband 30
I Don't Like… 32
Ready To Be Yours 34
Dear Father 37
Breath of Fresh Air 40
We Were Like 42
Stranger 44
Put You First 46
How Do You Feel at the End of the Day? 48
Real Talk 50
Issues of Life 52
A Wounded Heart 54
Don't Give Up For a "What If" 57
Love Don't Live Here Anymore 59
I Needed You Tonight 61
Can You See Me? 63
Say What You Mean 65
Invisible 67
To Be Loved 70
Whole Again 72
Do You Really Know Me? 74
Metamorphosis 77
Season of Uncertainty 80
No Fear Here 82
True Love 84
Forever in my Heart 86

Emotions

So Different	88
If Only	90
I'm Here For You	93
Jeanie in a Bottle	96
Everything	99
Am I Dreaming?	102
Thinking of You	105
Sleepless Night	107
The Meaning of Love	109
Be My Valentine	111
My Soul Mate	113
My Love For You	115
I Believe in Magic	118
True Friendship	121
If I Could Be Myself	124
Am I Forgiven?	127
Happiness…Agony	130
Let's Stay Together	140
Get to Know Me	142
Where Did You Go?	145
It's Going to be Alright	147
Special Bond	149
Make Up Your Mind	151
I Thought…	154
Silence	157
One Day at a Time	159
Miss Carrying You	162
In Love	165
I'm Here For You	167
Chosen	169
My True Love	171
Look To God	174
Let's Make it Work	176
A Part of You	180
About the Author	183

Emotions

Dedication

This book of poems is dedicated to the countless women that shared their stories and needed a voice.

These poems are associated with the love, joy, pain, hurt, sadness, forgiveness and complexity of what a woman goes through in a relationship.

It's our emotions expressed through what many are feeling and experiencing at that particular time in their life.

My prayer is that everyone was able to experience some relief and healing throughout their journey of love.

EMOTIONS

I feel every feeling, where should I begin?

Should I start with what I'm feeling now or from what I felt back then?

Then was in the past, so therefore I must let it go.

But these feelings inside that I'm feeling right now, I think that you should know.

Emotions bring forth commotion, because you can't always keep it within.

Frustration ends up in devastation, because it seems like there's no end.

No end to all of my problems that I face each and every day.

I cry deep down inside, because there seems like it's no way.

No way that I can be who I used to be. You have no idea how it hurts so much.

That I can't even embrace you with a hug or caress you with my touch.

To me, I always thought communication was the key.

To keep the relationship alive but it's hard for you to find 3 words to say to me.

Affection equals direction that leads you to romance.

Emotions

You had every opportunity, every advantage, and chance after chance.

To woo me, to love me, to do whatever you want with me.

Am I able to fit into your schedule? Let's say every Saturday around 3?

3 a.m. that is after we put the kids to sleep.

But then it's hush-hush and then rush-rush, because Sunday starts a new week.

Of church, then work, and then it's the same ole routine.

We go to work, we come home, you sleep while I cook and clean.

Depression makes me confess some of the hurt that I'm going through.

I'm mad then I'm saddened because my heart is longing for you.

Can't you see that I'm crying out through my silence and me being distant?

For instance, when you coime home I'm keeping busy or going to another room.

It's a deterrent and a distraction to keep from getting hurt by you.

I ponder every day. When will all of this end?

Emotions

I'm tired of playing the game. I no longer want to be that piece of your puzzle.

I QUIT……. you win.

I'm desperately trying to hold on and hang in there with all that I've got.

But there are many times where I say to myself, "I wish I had not."

Only because of all the hurt and discomfort that you put me through.

I'm at the point now to where I just don't know what to do.

I'm trying my best to be the perfect woman and stand by your side.

But I'm just not good enough, and I feel that I'm ruining your life.

Whatever I've done has completely shut you down.

I get no response from you, not a single word, and not even a sound.

You act as if I don't exist and that I'm not even here.

And that is the one thing that I dreaded and always feared.

That you'd lose your attraction, love, and interest in me.

Emotions

And that one day you'd pack up all your things and finally leave.

Now I'm at the point to where I feel myself shutting down.

I feel restricted, prohibited, and forceable bound.

I'm trying my hardest to do God's will, by holding steadfast and standing still.

I've stood so long now; I feel like I'm frozen.

It's like I'm numb, no willpower, no desire and no motive.

This is not the way I expected our relationship to be.

We're supposed to be excited, happy and carefree.

Oh, what I would give to have that again.

I just hope it's not too late. I just hope it's not the end.

WHERE DID THE LOVE GO?

You used to cuddle up and watch a movie with me, and now you don't.

You used to talk to me until the wee hours of the night, and now you won't.

You used to be affectionate with me, but now you push me away.

You used to come home early enough to see me,

but now I get a glimpse of you at the end of the day.

You used to be romantic by sending me cards and beautiful flowers,

but now I don't see you or hear from you for hours.

You used to be fun, spontaneous and adventurous,

but now you act heartless, cold and suspicious.

Am I really becoming that much of a bore? Is coming home to me becoming like a chore?

Do you really know that I'm hurting inside?

I wish things can go back to being the same as far back as when I first told you my name.

Those were the days when I was special for you. Those are the memories I don't want to lose.

Emotions

How did things get so off track? Will we ever get our relationship back?

Just to let you know I pray every night, and I pray every day,

that our love for one another

doesn't go astray.

Emotions

IN MY FEELINGS

I have feelings of hurt, pain, anger, sadness, loneliness, abandonment, neglect,

betrayal, bitterness, hate, fear and rage.

But on the other hand: I love you; I adore you, I cherish you, I miss you, I want you,

I need you, and I'm so confused.

My emotions are mixed, my feelings are distorted, and my mind is a blank.

I have so much going through my head, that it's hard for me to think.

I wish I knew how I could handle this situation.

Because I'm tired of always being upset and frustrated.

I don't even think I have any more tears to cry.

Due to all of the anger that you can see through my eyes.

I keep all of my problems bottled up inside.

And when I finally explode you wonder why.

It's because you never give me a chance to tell you how I really feel.

I have so many wounds inside that I've never let completely heal.

If you can only put that covering back over my head.

Emotions

I don't think things would be this bad.

You're under God and I'm under you now. It's up to you to show me what to do.

A sanctified man will sanctify his wife.

If you can just stay in your word and bring me back my life.

A life of love, happiness, no worries and no fears.

No more hurt, pain and nights of endless and flowing tears.

Emotions

HOME ALONE

It's another lonely evening and your still not home.

It's another sad night and I feel all alone.

I waited all day and all night for you to call our phone.

Whenever I picked it up all I heard was a dial tone.

Hoping that you would be on the other end.

Then I said to myself, "Who am I pretending?"

I have to convince myself that it won't always be like this.

And that some day we will get back our marital bliss.

I never thought when we got married that we'd be so far apart.

The only thing I can do now is just keep you close to my heart.

And hopefully you can do the same for me.

Because I know you'll be home eventually.

Emotions

MUCH TOO BUSY FOR ME

You're in a world of your own and it's bad, because I'm not in it.

Your time has been consumed and you're too occupied in handling your business.

You walked passed me today without giving me a kiss.

I wore my new outfit today, "Do you like it?"

It's funny because you noticed your DVD was out of it's case.

And that your razor was put in another place.

Have you noticed lately that I really need you?

Probably not, because other things and other people are more important to you.

Whatever happened to "Cleave to your wife?"

Who gave you the authority to end my life?

I'm longing to live Happily Ever After.

I guess at the end of the book, I need to add another chapter.

To explain to people how their life really can be, if you marry someone who's always busy.

Emotions

IN MEMORY OF

I died today, and you didn't even notice it.

I lost all self worth, and decided to call it quits.

I'm laying in my bed, otherwise known as my grave.

Barricaded by the side walls of my casket, wishing that my life could've been saved.

The covers are over my head, just as if my casket were closed.

It's just like it was when I was alive, full of darkness and bitter cold.

I never thought this was how life would be.

I think I'm better off living in eternity.

There I would have no worries, not stress, no hurts nor pains.

I'd be happy and free and have my life back again.

Emotions

NOTICE ME

What can I do to get your attention and show you that exist

Should I get breast implants, a stomach reduction, or add collagen to my lips?

What's got you so preoccupied to where you don't know if I'm here or there?

Do you notice I'm crying every night?

Or is it that you just don't care?

Can you see that I'm trying to reach out to you?

Can you see me stretching out my hands?

I'd rather be embraced in your arms, than to be caressed by another man.

Will you please stop and take a minute to take a glance or a long look at me?

Because this may be your last chance to see how unhappy you've made me.

Emotions

WHERE ARE YOU?

You stated you're unhappy, well now that makes two of us.

Then you suddenly want to make love but now I don't want to be touched.

You come and you go daily, as if you have two personalities.

I don't know who you are one day after the next.

Is this some kind of game you're playing or is this reality?

Your feelings are turned off and on like a light switch, for me it's hard to believe.

Or were your feelings and emotions at the bottom of your sleeves.

Who is the man that I am with? Because you're definitely not the one I married.

It feels like I'm living with a stranger, and sometimes that feeling is so scary.

I don't know which of your "persons" that I'm supposed to attack.

I just wish you'd make it a little easier for me to get my husband back.

Emotions

WHY ME?

Why did I involve myself with someone who didn't share the same goals as me?

Why did I marry someone who didn't even want a family?

Was it the lust that we shared or was there some form of chemistry?

It was something there for us to say, "I do", and vow to be together for eternity.

Now everything I wanted out of life is either gone or has been placed on hold.

I'll never have the opportunity to achieve my desires, my wishes, and my goals.

But now I get to sit back and watch you do everything you always wanted to do.

I guess this is all I get out of being married to you.

Emotions

IDEAL HUSBAND

Heaven sent you to find a wife and then obtain favor from the Lord.

Understanding to his wife's every need. And makes sure she's loved, cherished, and adored.

Supportive in her every decision she makes, also in her desires and goals.

Believes in her and is there for her, until death or until she grows old.

A confident, a friend, a spiritual guide, as well as my lover.

Nevertheless, his one and only, because of me there should be no other.

Dependable, Reliable, Trustworthy and Honest in every way. Who is special in my eyes, as well as God's, and stay the same person every day.

Emotions

I DON'T LIKE…

I don't like to be looked at as a prize or trophy in your showcase.

I don't like to be considered your dime piece or just a pretty face.

I don't like to pretend that we're living such a wonderful life.

I don't like the fact that you can't even treat me like your wife.

I don't like to know that I will never be put first.

I don't like when you make me feel insecure and even hurt.

I don't like it when you try and dictate my every move.

I don't like seeing that everything I love…….I lose.

I don't like hearing that you've been unhappy and stressed.

But most of all I hate knowing that our marriage is such a mess.

Emotions

READY TO BE YOURS

I once was like a caterpillar, who one day blossomed into a beautiful butterfly.

But once God entered into my life, he changed me: like I went through a process of metamorphosis.

And peace then entered within. That peace suddenly brought forth trials and tribulations that I had to one day overcome.

My life felt as if it were twists and turns brought forth stress points of sadness, depression, anxiety and disappointment.

I finally overcame the obstacles that were put forth in my path. I was happy again because the eye of God was upon me.

This has helped me to better myself and make me intricate in detail as the red rose.

Its sweet smell has made my attitude, temper, and personality sweet as well.

The dome symbolizes the House of God in which I was under to protect me from the evil forces of the outside world.

It's also the place that helped me keep my sanity. And is also the place where someday I will wed and be at peace.

Emotions

Which will enable me to be the woman that I am and be looked upon as a positive image in the eyes of God and my family.

Emotions

Emotions

DEAR FATHER

If you hear my voice, please answer this silent prayer.

My heart, my soul, and my innermost thoughts with you I will share.

Some nights I often cry myself to sleep.

All of the thoughts running through my mind are so extreme and so deep.

Dear Father, please release some of this agonizing pressure that's locked up in my mind.

And help me search for whatever it is that I'm supposed to find.

I can't stay focused because my head constantly spins.

I tried to walk the walk and fight the fight, but I never seem to win.

Is what you're putting me through a test?

Will I be left behind or caught up with you and the rest?

Lord, please answer this silent prayer. I'm asking you once again.

Please mold me and shape me and prepare me for the end.

Lord give me some wisdom, knowledge, understanding and strength.

Emotions

And help me to believe that in your word is what you said and also what you meant.

Lord, I want to be caught up and raptured in the end.

So please forgive me for all of my wrongdoings and save me again.

Emotions

BREATH OF FRESH AIR

I was your breath of fresh air when you came out of a relationship that went bad.

I was your breath of fresh air that you always wish you had.

I was your breath of fresh air that got you through some hard times.

I was your breath of fresh air that erased the bad memories from your mind

I was your breath of fresh air that soothed you through the night.

I was your breath of fresh air that made everything feel alright.

I was your breath of fresh air that would never leave.

So go ahead and exhale my love. It's okay now, because you can finally breathe.

WE WERE LIKE

We were like the Will and Jada of old times.

We were always together and stuck by one another's side.

We were like the Beyonce and Jay Z, a prissy thug and a bad boy from the hood.

All anyone could ever say about our relationship was that it was "All good."

We were like the Foxy Brown and Master P on t.v. and film.

They way I caught you staring at me made me feel jittery inside, and I

couldn't help but glance at you at a whim.

We were like everyone it seemed, but what about the "me and you?"

In the beginning it was like all of this was too good to be true.

But what would it be like if we were together?

Is it a chance that you would risk or take?

Would it be filled with love, romance, and laughter?

Will there be disappointments, pain and heartache?

What would it be like if we were like us?

Emotions

STRANGER

Hey there stranger. Where have you been?

I've been asking all around if anyone has seen my friend.

Quite some time has passed, and I stopped searching for you.

I had to move on with my life. Where do I begin?

What do I do?

It's like you magically disappeared in the middle of thin air.

Now what was I supposed to do? What you did was so unfair.

I can hear you say. "Deal with it, let it go and move on."

It's so easy for you to say, and it's easier said than done.

All I knew and had was you, and without you I have been incomplete.

Now you're the stranger that I dream about whenever I go to sleep.

Emotions

Emotions

PUT YOU FIRST

It's extremely important to remember to put yourself first.

Because only you know what you want and what it is that you deserve.

Don't let life pass you by without doing something for you.

It's your time to rise and do what it is you have to do.

We tend to get caught up in the hustle and bustle of life,

and forget about ourselves.

Then we end up putting our time and energy into something or someone else.

So, take some time to reflect on your wants and your needs,

before your mind explodes or your heart burst.

Figure out what it is that's important to you and remember to put you first.

Emotions

HOW DO YOU FEEL AT THE END OF THE DAY

How do you feel at the end of the day?

Are you happy or are you sad?

It's time to make some grown up decisions, or you'll regret that you never had.

It's important that you have outweighed the good and the bad in every incident and situation.

Find out what it is that keeps your heart filled with so much frustration.

Get down on your knees and pray and seek God like never before.

Wait until he gives you confirmation then you'll know that your answer came from the Lord.

Now that you got your questions answered when you got down on your knees to pray.

You can finally answer the question…..

How do you feel at the end of the day?

Emotions

REAL TALK

When you say what's on your mind and express how you feel.

You leave the listener no choice to accept the fact that you're keeping it real.

Sometimes the truth hurts, so if it cuts then let it bleed.

At least now you know the facts and sometimes the facts are hard to receive.

Let the truth be told and accept it in your heart and also in your mind.

Forget all the sugar coating and beating around the bush, let the truth be what you find.

So, if you're going to be real, then act the part and walk the walk.

Open up` your ears and be receptive to the one who engages in real talk.

Emotions

ISSUES OF LIFE

Can there ever be a day of just tranquility and peace?

Can there ever be a night when I can get at least eight hours of sleep?

Will I ever be able to utter the words "Everything will be alright?"

If things were that easy there would be no issues of life.

Will there ever be a morning without frustration and anxiety?

Will I ever experience an afternoon without shouting and fighting?

Is there such an evening when I can just lay down and relax?

Do you think I'm at the point where I'm at my max?

Do you think I have enough strength to stand up and fight against the test and trials that's

a part of my issues of life?

In the midst of my issues of life I ask, "Where are you God?"

Do you think he's listening? Will he answer my prayers?

Please God fix my issues of life, so that I'll no longer be scared.

Emotions

Emotions

A WOUNDED HEART

Where should I begin? Where should I start?

Let me tell you about the story of my wounded heart.

It all started when I felt I wasn't needed.

When everything in my life suddenly depleted.

When all of my goals were never completed.

And when I felt all used up and mistreated.

Come along with me on the journey we're about to embark.

On the story I'm sharing about my wounded heart.

It all got worse when I started to feel all alone.

And had to express myself through poetry or song.

I felt there was no place for me, I didn't fit in, nor did I belong.

I felt completely empty inside because you were always gone.

I had many restless nights trying to preoccupy myself with something to do.

So, I pulled out my pen and paper and started to expound on the truth.

The truth about a major part on how I ended up with a wounded heart.

Emotions

My wounds are wide open. They have not scabbed up or healed.

It's like open heart surgery without anesthesia; the pain is unreal.

How long will this go on? Will we have to depart,

In order for me to not have a wounded heart?

I remember a time when I was the cream of the crop.

My heart is so wounded, it's no longer beating.

It has now stopped.

Emotions

DON'T GIVE UP FOR A "WHAT IF"

Don't give up for a what if, because you don't know what the outcome will be.

Will it be hell on earth or pure romance and chemistry?

What if you thought the person would be like the one you know years ago?

What if they were still the person that you loved, appreciated and adored?

Would you be willing to proceed with the one your committed to?

Or go back to the one that I knew before you?

LOVE DON'T LIVE HER ANYMORE

Love don't live here anymore. My question is "Where has it gone?"

Love don't live here anymore. Why, when, and where did it all go wrong?

Love don't live here anymore. It's been gone a long while.

Love don't live here anymore. And with it, it took our happiness and smiles.

Love don't live here anymore. At times I wish it could've stayed.

Love don't live here anymore. It looks like it just got up and walked away.

Love don't live here anymore. Because I no longer feel complete.

Love got up and split and left me in pain and feeling defeat.

Looks like love is never coming back; therefore, I must move on.

I remember when love used to live here, and it saddens me now that it's gone.

Emotions

Emotions

I NEEDED YOU TONIGHT

I needed you tonight and you weren't even there.

I don't understand how you could be so insensitive, and act like you don't even care.

Today I dot the worse news that I'd never thought I would receive.

I needed you tonight and you weren't there to comfort me.

I didn't have you to hold my hand nor could I cry on your shoulder.

I needed you tonight, and you didn't bother to come over.

I tried several times to contact you by text and by phone.

I needed you tonight, but you left me all alone.

I finally saw you tonight after hours of being gone.

You didn't greet me or console me nor did you ask me what was wrong.

I needed you tonight, and at the same time I didn't want to come home.

You'll never know I needed you tonight unless you ever read this poem.

Emotions

CAN YOU SEE ME?

Can you even see me? Do I exist in your eyes?

I'm sitting right here. Can you say hello when you walk through the door?

And when you leave can you say good-bye?

Hello!!!! I'm right here is there something you missed?

You walked right past me without giving me a hug or a kiss.

I don't know what it is that bothers me the most.

Whether it be acting like you don't care or treating me as if I were a ghost.

Can you even see me? Just in case you didn't know I'm alive.

I'm still the mother of our children, and the last time I checked I was still your wife.

I really don't believe you can see me, nor do I believe you think I exist.

All I ask is that you acknowledge me, can you please grant me that wish?

Can you see me now? Can you see that I'm all alone?

Let's try it again.... Can you see me????

No. Not anymore, because now I am gone.

Emotions

SAY WHAT YOU MEAN

Say what you mean and mean what you say.

Because if you don't get it together, it's going to be too late.

You can never seem to be able to tell me the truth.

I trust nothing you say, therefore I need proof.

You always have some fable to tell each and every day.

All I ask is for you to say what you mean and mean what you say.

You're often gone for hours at a time and when you return,

you come up with such and unbelievable lie.

I don't know why you just don't stay away.

Because you'll never say what you mean and mean what you say.

Emotions

INVISIBLE

I'm so confused right now. Is there something I missed?

Did he just look right through me as if I didn't exist?

A quick "Hey!" is the only word I got.

Maybe I can get a kiss or hug if I just stand up.

Wow! Did he just turn and walk away?

No greeting from him after being gone from me 19 hours today.

My heart is rapidly beating, my head is pounding, and the tears

are swelling up inside.

Momentarily I became a mute and swallowed my pride.

A soft whisper came to my head. "A soft answer turns away wrath."

Back to my wifely duties I went, and I poured in the bubbles for his bath.

I've come to the conclusion that I'll never advance from the bottom of the totem pole.

After 17 years! I'm still there at the bottom! I just don't GET IT! This perplexes my soul.

I never knew that in a marriage that this would even be permissible.

Emotions

To be with someone that would always treat me as if I were invisible.

Emotions

TO BE LOVED

Take me as I am or watch me as I walk away.

Though our outward man perishes yet the inward man is renewed day by day.

You have to live your life today day by day, because life is too short.

Never give up, be encouraged.

Sadness, disappointment and despair have to flee in the presence of hope.

A woman's heart should be so deep into the Lord,

that a man should have to seek him first even to find her.

Keep your mind stayed on him, and he will keep you in perfect peace.

It's so harder to forgive people that aren't even sorry.

Stick with love because hate is to great a burden to bear.

And just pray that one day you will have a love that the two of you can share.

WHOLE AGAIN

It finally feels like I'm breathing for the very first time.

Today I was able to exhale and open up my eyes.

I have go keep telling myself that there will be no more tears this way again.

I now know who it is that I need, and that's God he is my only true friend.

We allow the issues of life to consume us and overshadow our minds.

I'm not going to let this happen again, I promise it's the last time.

You can doubt me if you want to, don't worry you just watch and see.

I'm going to let God change and transform myself into a brand new me.

DO YOU REALLY KNOW ME?

If I'd ask you what my favorite color is you'd probably say red.

That's when I'd look at you in disgust with utter disappointment and shake my head.

Do you really know me? That's the question I sometimes ask.

For you to learn me and understand me, isn't really a hard task.

I'm quite simple, a plain Jane type of girl.

I'd rather go for walks and receive roses, than an elaborate trip around the world.

Just in case you don't know, here's a little taste of me.

I'd prefer going to a romantic dinner, than sitting at home watching t.v.

And just for the record my favorite color isn't red, it's black.

It's that simple! Things that I thought you would notice and see.

That's why I sometimes ask myself. "Does he really know me?"

My favorite food is seafood, with pasta being my second choice.

Emotions

Did you even know I could sing? I have such a wonderful voice.

I enjoy reading, walking, holding hands in the park.

I adore watching the sunset and clouds, but I dread being alone in the dark.

I love to dance and listening to the sound of the wind blowing through the trees.

Now after getting just a little taste.

The question I ask you is, "Do you really know me?"

Emotions

METAMORPHOSIS

What a profound transformation we've made during this time together.

We've gone through so much turmoil in this relationship and years of stormy weather.

From the extreme dynamics of misunderstanding and lack of communication.

Sometimes issues being brushed under the rug without closure or explanation.

Just like a caterpillar becoming a butterfly, our relationship shifted from one place to another.

Sometimes disagreements weren't even worth the fight, most times I didn't even bother.

Bother to talk about the things that were bothering me, like not feeling loved or at times often seen.

But with continuous prayer and putting all our trust and faith in God, He finally started to remove those obstacle we kept stumbling upon.

We've had so much more growth that outweighed the challenges and perspectives.

We began to have more understanding with one another and our communication became much more effective.

We were learning how to better understand and support each other's emotional needs.

Emotions

The more time we spent together helped us understand one another.

And our connection most certainly strengthened indeed.

We figured out how to move from destructive arguments to honest constructive communication.

Which deepened out emotional and physical intimacy as well as our trust and admiration.

Life's transitions forced us to adapt to major changes in our relationship and life.

It changed when we had children and as we matured, while learning what it meant to be husband and wife.

We were evolving individually and becoming more vulnerable to one another.

It allowed us to become better friends and have a stronger connection as lovers.

This new self-discovery took us on a journey that we thought we'd never see.

I'm so glad we went through this metamorphosis together versus trying to figure it our separately.

You are my person, as I am yours and I'm thankful that God placed us together.

Now I look forward to spending the rest of my life with you and staying married happily ever after.

SEASON OF UNCERTAINTY

Many of us are in an uncertain season that God has allowed to take place.

We must have faith and trust in him, and continue to run this race.

God has ordained this season, which caused many of us to surrender our will.

We need to allow God to have his way, and continue to stand and be still.

So let's trust in God and not in people, because they cannot solve our problems.

Just keep the faith, because God loves you, and just wants you to keep trusting him.

Remember this is just a test for us, so don't doubt God for any reason.

Put your uncertainty in God's hands, and he will help you through this season.

Emotions

Emotions

NO FEAR HERE

There is nothing to fear but fear itself.

Until you get diagnosed with a condition that affects your health.

We often take it for granted and think we're healthier than ever.

Don't say it couldn't happen to you.

Remember to never say never.

It's imperative that you have to begin taking care of yourself.

We get so caught up in our fancy cars, our appearances, and our wealth.

God had the final say so, and is the finisher of our faith.

We must re-evaluate our lives, and if you haven't already you may want to start today.

There's no need to have any fear, just cast all your cares upon him.

And if you do so, I guarantee He'll deliver you in the end.

Emotions

TRUE LOVE

Whatever it is that you're going thought remember that God will always see you through.

Sometimes we go through so much hurt and pain,

But there will be a rainbow at the end of your rain.

We must cast all of our cares and give our problems to the Lord.

In doing so, he will allow us to receive our reward.

Victory and happiness is what we will get.

Once we open up our hearts and learn to forgive.

In all that you're going through count it all joy.

Don't get consumed with negative thinking, or else your heart will be destroyed.

Don't let a hardened heart cause you to fall.

But remember this…….. True love does conquer all.

Emotions

FOREVER IN MY HEART

I can never talk to you without asking the question why.

"Why did you leave me out on the cliff, hanging there to die?

We were as one for one moment in time.

I thought that I'd always be yours, and that you'd always be mine.

I didn't beg you to stay with me, I wasn't holding you by your sleeve.

You made that final decision and decided that you wanted to leave.

After leaving me in this world with no one to call my own,

I finally felt what it feels like to be left all alone.

You cannot escape these feelings, because it's so strong in your heart.

You'll soon come to the realization that you need me, now that we're apart.

So, take your time, please take all of the time in the world.

Because you'll always be my baby, just like I'll always be your girl.

Emotions

SO DIFFERENT

You're in your world living life to the fullest.

I'm in my world dreaming about living a life like yours.

You're in your world taking care of business and steadily growing.

I'm in my world trying to get some business yet steadily dying.

You're in your world thriving and succeeding.

I'm in my world struggling and constantly failing.

You're in your world living your dreams.

I'm in my world still dreaming my dreams.

We're two different people from two different times.

In two different worlds with two different minds.

If Only...

Emotions

IF ONLY…

If you could only read my mind and hear my innermost thoughts.

You would soon be aware that I feel all of this was my fault.

If only I wouldn't have gotten mad at you for ruining our plans.

You wouldn't be in this predicament with broken legs, arms, and fractured hands.

If only I could've called you to tell you that I was alright.

You wouldn't be laying there in the hospital on these cold and dreary night.

If only I could've paged you and told you to come tomorrow,

all of these people in the waiting room wouldn't be feeling all of this sorrow.

If only I could've told you to pull over to the side of the street,

you wouldn't be laying there with stimulants hooked up to both of your feet.

If only I could've been there to tell you to slow down, that tree

Emotions

would've still been standing and not uprooted from the ground.

If only I could've told you that I'd come see you soon, maybe this could've

happened to me instead of you.

Emotions

I'M HERE FOR YOU

As I sit here waiting, contemplating about the outcome of our situation.

I'm having feelings of anger, hurt, pain and total devastation.

Never in a million years would I expect something so tragic to happen to you.

I couldn't even prepare myself, now I'm left confused not knowing what to do.

While I watch you laying there so helpless, but yet so content.

I can't help but to remenis about all of the times that we spent.

Countless conversations, deep discussions, and serious talks.

Numerous movies, dinners, shopping and not to mention our midnight walks.

Oh, how I miss all of that bliss. The warmth of your embrace the cuddling,

and the sweet soft kisses from your lips.

These past few days have been so crucial to me.

I cannot eat, I can't stop crying, nor can I sleep.

Emotions

There's nothing else that I can do except for to sit back and pray.

And hope that you continue to recover day by day.

I just want to let you know that I'm here with you until the end.

Not because I'm that special someone in your life, but because

I'm your best friend.

JEANIE IN A BOTTLE

On that final day when you open your eyes, I hope to your surprise

you find me standing by your side.

With tears in my eyes and a smile on my face.

With outstretched arms waiting for your warm embrace.

I will wait on you hand and foot, or even foot and hand.

I'm your servant, I'm your Jeanie, your every wish is my command.

Just say it, I'll do it. Just ask and it's done.

I'll be both your arms and your legs, because together we are one.

What more can you ask for besides someone like me? Who's willing to go that extra mile,

And be all that you want me to be.

I'll be you rehabilitator, your physical therapist, your doctor, and your nurse.

I'll stop whatever it is that I am doing only to put you first.

I was put into your life for a reason, I'm not here by mistake.

Emotions

I'm your sunshine, your burst of energy. I'm what makes your feel great.

When all of this is over, we can just look back and see.

How I was there for you and cared for you during your time of need.

I consider this a blessing that has helped us to become more close.

That is the only wish of mine, my only desire, and my only hope.

I don't think you understand how deeply you've been missed.

I'm just glad that I could be of some help, and that Jeanie to grant your every wish.

Emotions

EVERYTHING

It's all because of you, I'm never sad and blue. You brighten up my days in your own special way. Whenever your around, I'm never feeling down. You are a trusted friend, In you I can depend.

If I were to write a song, it would be called "EVERYTHING".

Because you are everything and everything is you.

It may not mean anything now, but all of it is true.

I've been missing you so much during the time we've been apart.

But the memories that I have to you remain close to my heart.

I don't know while you've been away if you've been thinking of me.

I just hope the feeling that you used to have are the same as they used to be.

You probably thought I forgot about you, but believe me that's not the case.

I had to give you some time to decide what you wanted,

so therefore, I had to wait.

But the waiting was torture, and the torture brought forth pain.

Emotions

I honestly felt that I was completely going insane.

I'd never thought that you would have such an effect on me.

I was cranky, I was moody, and at times evil as can be.

But things had to change. I couldn't be that way forever.

Because I know there would soon come a day that we will soon be together.

Emotions

Emotions

AM I DREAMING?

It all happened during dinner it was a rather special occasion.

I felt a little nervous, but at the same time I felt very elated.

I sat there pondering what this could be all about.

"Is he going to pop the big question?"

I thought even harder, then I began to have my doubts.

The conversation we had, had me quite suspicious.

He talked of our past, present and future. Then he asked how I felt about children.

He wanted to know what would make our relationship even happier.

He said. "Living happily forever with you, is the only thing I'm after."

I answered all of his questions and openly and honestly as I could.

Then he was going to ask his next question, but we were interrupted by the waiter

right before he said. "Would.....

His sincerity and courage had me so amazed, then he pulled out this small box and asked.

Emotions

"Are you ready to be engaged?"

I was so overwhelmed that I could do nothing but cry.

He pulled out his handkerchief and began wiping the tears from my eyes.

I looked into his eyes and repeatedly told him yes.

He said. "That was the answer that I had guessed."

Then he placed the ring on the fourth finger of my left hand.

And told me to pick out my maid of honor, because he had already chosen his best man.

He asked me to marry him! This is so hard to believe.

Well of course it was because I woke up and realized that if was only a dream.

Extremely disappointed because this was the next level in our relationship to begin.

For richer or for poorer, till death do we part was the only way it was supposed to end.

THINKING OF YOU

Waking up in the morning, I seem to think of only you.

When I hear the wind blow, I hear you calling my name.

Like the soft subtle sounds from a bass guitar.

When I hear the birds chirp, I hear you whispering sweet words in my ear.

When I see the sun shining, I feel the warmth of the sunrays embracing me.

Like it was your arms wrapped around my body.

When I look into the mirror, I see your face instead of mine.

Almost as if we were staring into each other's eyes.

Emotions

SLEEPLESS NIGHT

It's the middle of the night and I cannot sleep.

I'm tossing and turning, staring at the clock watching the time pass by.

Feeling a sense of loneliness, because you're not here beside me.

Anxious because of the sound of the telephone ringing.

Just to pick it up knowing you're not on the other end.

My eyelids are growing heavy, but I won't close my eyes.

Because I will only dream about you.

Only to wake up and see you're nowhere to be found.

The Meaning of Love

THE MEANING OF LOVE

What is love? Love is a feeling that two people share when they care for one another.

It's an emotion that is spiritual, physical, and inspirational.

Showing love and saying you love someone is two different things.

Like seeing is to believing, as believing is to seeing, and doing is to saying,

like saying is to doing.

Showing love is expressing it. Saying you love someone is meaning it.

Believing in love is wanting it.

Doing it, is self-explanatory.

Love is a strong and meaningful word that shouldn't be taken lightly.

And it is such a beautiful experience.

But for love to be such a beautiful thing, why is it so hard to give?

BE MY VALENTINE

It's hard to find the words to express the way that I feel.

The only thing that I know how to do best, is just to keep it real.

The feelings that I have for you are so difficult to explain.

Sometimes I just want to say it out loud, but other times I think it's best

to keep it within.

I can never get you out of my mind, because you remain so close to my heart.

So, let's forget about the past, become better acquainted, and get a fresh new start.

I think you have a general idea of what I'm trying to say.

I want you to be my valentine from now on after today.

Emotions

MY SOUL MATE

When we were born, the soul that we were given splits apart.

And the other half is given to someone else.

So all of our lives we're looking for the person with the other half.

When we finally find that other half, our soul says

"At last, I can rest."

I have finally found my soul mate, my better half.

When we first met, I recognized you, and felt the other part of my soul

Coming complete.

When we first met, I automatically knew you were my better half. MY SOUL MATE.

Now on this day, let's think about becoming one.

Emotions

MY LOVE FOR YOU

As the tears stream down my face, as my heart breaks into two.

I can't help but to think about the pain that you put me through.

I promised myself that I wouldn't be hurt again. We weren't even lovers

just supposedly friends.

But that friendship grew into something that turned into a little bit more.

I expressed my feelings, but yours you ignored.

It left me confused not knowing what to do.

I couldn't stand the fact that I was slowly loosing you.

As I lay here thinking, better yet reminiscing about the times that we spent together.

I was hoping and praying that our relationship would last forever and ever.

We had good times and bad times, and many ups and downs.

They were what I considered experiences that turned my life around.

Experiences that helped me to grow, to learn, and to understand.

Emotions

What this word is we call love.

I can't bear to be hurt again.

I BELIEVE IN MAGIC

I never believed in magic until the day I met you.

It was like hocus-pocus, abra-Cadabra, and you appeared into my life.

NOW THAT'S MAGIC!

I said I wanted someone, a companion, someone to spend time with.

and to care about.

I believed someone would come and before I knew it,

and there you were. NOW THAT'S MAGIC!

Who'd ever think I'd believe in magic, but it really works.

I can think about you until I get the visual image of your face.

It's like you're with me all day long. NOW THAT'S MAGIC!

When you kiss me, I melt.

When you touch me, I melt.

When you hold me, I melt.

Which makes me disappear into a world consisting of only you and I.

And when your soft lips brush ever so softly on that secret spot on my neck.

Emotions

I reappear to the present state of me and you.

In and out, out and it, disappearing, reappearing…..NOW THAT'S MAGIC!

The way that you make me feel and the feelings you stir up inside.

The tip of your hat, the poke of your wand, the motion of your body,

and the stroke of your hand.

NOW THAT'S MAGIC!

That can turn into a magical experience that we both can share together.

TRUE FRIENDSHIP

I thank the Lord for giving me such a wonderful friend like you.

Who was there for me and cared for me when I was going through.

Through the good days and bad days, through all of my ups and downs.

I know whenever I needed someone you were always there to be found.

To hear my complaints, to feeling pain, to hear my laughter and cries.

To give me encouraging words, to give me a hug, and to wipe the tears from my eyes.

But now it's time to flip the script and turn it the other way around.

I'm here for you, to encourage you, now that you're feeling down.

I can hear it in your voice, I can see it in your eyes, that something's terribly wrong.

Something was bothering you, you tried to hide it, but I knew it all along.

So why don't you tell me what it is that's laying so heavily on your mind.

Emotions

Whatever it is you will overcome it. If not, I think it's something together we can fight.

By communicating with me by sharing with me, all of your pain and hurt.

You never know if you talk about it. It may go away.

Let's try it. It may even work.

God knows your trouble if you never tell me, just do his will and follow his commands.

There's nothing else that I can do except to pray and put it in his hands.

It really saddens me to see you this way, and to see the disappointment in your eyes.

My heart is heavy because I can feel your pain, and I feel as if I were going to cry.

Even though you're not here with me in the flesh, you're here with me in my heart.

So just hold your hands close to your heart; feel me there and know that I'll never depart.

If that doesn't make you smile, I don't know what will.

So just keep happy thoughts of me.

So you can relax and of course be comfortable, but most of all in perfect peace.

Emotions

IF I COULD BE MYSELF

If I could only be myself, I wouldn't have to keep everything Inside.

If I could only be myself, my emotions and feelings, I would no longer have to hide.

If I could only be myself, our friendship would've probably gotten stronger.

If I could only be myself, our relationship would have probably lasted longer.

If I could only be myself, our conversations wouldn't have to end so early in the night.

If I could only be myself, whenever I'm around you I wouldn't have to feel so uptight.

If I could only be myself, I could joke around without you taking it to the extreme.

If I could only be myself, I could tease you without you thinking I were being mean.

If I could only be myself, whenever I made a comment, you wouldn't think I was being funny.

If I could only be myself, I could call you my sweetie, my baby, or even my honey.

If I could only be myself, I wouldn't have this feeling that I was being fake.

Emotions

If I could only be myself, I could tell you that us coming together was no mistake.

If I could only be myself, I could tell you that inside I feel so alone.

If I could only be myself, I could tell you face-to-face, instead of writing it in this poem.

AM I FORGIVEN

I'm sorry for the hurt and pain that I may have put you through.

But have you thought that I may be going through the same thing too?

I've apologized to you over and over again.

But you won't accept my apology or try to be my friend.

You're not the only one in the world who is going through some things.

That's just part of the test and trials that life sometimes bring.

I know things seemed like they were moving rather fast,

when we should've taken it more slow.

But neither one of us said anything, instead we went with the flow.

The flow was moving rather steadily, the chemistry seemed to be just right.

So, I didn't put up a fight, because it was such a delight to reach that height.

Just to be in your presence was such a wonderful sight.

I felt free as a bird, and as high as a kite.

Emotions

To wake up with you in the morning, to open up my eyes to see you in the sunlight.

To look outside in that sky, at the clouds that were so white.

To go to sleep at night with your body wrapped around me so tight.

I never would've imagined, but I thought that you might be the one that I end up with.

But I guess my thinking wasn't so bright.

So please don't give up on me, or on us so fast.

Instead let's start over, maybe this time we will last.

As friends instead of enemies, as buddies instead of being intimate with me.

Whether you want to or not, you'll always be a part of me.

There's not a day that goes by that I don't think of you since we've been apart.

I just want to let you know that you'll always have that special place in my heart.

Emotions

Emotions

HAPPINESS…..AGONY

I thought I'd write you this simple poem to express the way that I feel.

It's hard to explain what I'm feeling inside, so I'll do my best to keep it real.

It all started back when I was a teen, and feeling so all alone.

When no one was there for me, or cared for me, or even acknowledged

who I was.

But one Sunday morning in December of "93" we were introduced one another.

From that day as I had a feeling inside that we were meant to be together.

After talking on the phone almost every day to the wee hours of the night.

The feelings of love I thought I never had started growing stronger inside.

In a way it scared me, and I got so confused, so I started

to push you away.

But deep down inside that's not what I wanted, so I tried my best to get you to stay.

Emotions

You were a blessing to me, a miracle, like an angel sent from above.

To give me attention, to spend quality time, but most of all show me some love.

The wall that I built around my heart where no one else could get close to.

It started to tumble down every moment and second that I talked

or even spent with you.

I soon became interested and wanted to see what you were all about.

So, I let down my guard and opened up my heart. Then I gave you the benefit of the doubt.

Things were running smoothly, and time passed by that's when things started to change.

The person that I cared for and thought that I knew, no longer remained the same.

So, I felt all these years that we were together was nothing but a waste of time.

Not only did you break my heart, but you played with my emotions and

also played with my mind.

I tried and tried to work things out, but you constantly pushed me away.

Emotions

You never really told me the real reason why, I guess it's because you were afraid.

Afraid of the commitment, afraid to be hurt, afraid of what the outcome may be.

Only if you would've just believed in your heart, or even believed in me.

If you would've believed that I was the one who was made for you, and the one

who would treat you right.

Who'd be by your side, love and cared for you every single day and night.

I guess you just weren't ready to settle down and devote all of your time to me.

You'd rather spend all of your time with your friends and be the player you wanted to be.

All of our conversations ended in arguments which left me rather upset.

You had made me so mad, that I started to hate you and regret the day we first met.

As we finally separated and wounds slowly began to heal, I was hit by another surprise.

All that time that I thought you cared for me was just one big lie.

Emotions

Then I really started missing you and desperately wanted to see you, and haven't talked

to you in a very long while.

You told me you missed me and wanted to be with me, but failed to mention that

someone was having your child.

You asked me to come over to discuss the situation, and I asked was it true

and the whole thing you tried to deny.

You finally confessed and to the truth, and I felt weak in the knees but

held back the river of tears in my eyes.

What was it about me that you didn't like that caused you to turn to someone else?

I was the one you said you cared about; you said I was your "Baby Girl!"

I mean, you told me all of this yourself. I was totally devasted, but I had to move on

because things weren't going to change.

The person I thought I knew and that had love for me, the feelings were no longer the same.

I decided to stay away from you for a very long time, and build that brick

Emotions

wall back around my heart.

And wouldn't let anyone else break it down ever since we've been apart.

I met new people and began to date, then I started to get confronted.

With marriage proposals and long-term commitments, but I already knew

who it was that I wanted.

It was very hard to let you go completely, but I knew I had to move on.

It was difficult for me to get close to someone else, because it was you that I always adored.

I thought maybe if we tried to be friends then everything would be cool.

But once again you started to doubt me and made me look like a fool.

All of the mixed signals that you kept giving me was hard to comprehend.

Until late one night a little bird told me, that you were in a secret relationship with

one of my so-called friends.

I never thought you would stoop so low to hurt me even more.

Emotions

I guess it's just that you had nothing better to do, or maybe because you were simply bored.

It felt like a stinging slap in my face and a deadly stab in my back.

I could never understand in a million years how you could hurt me like that.

So once again my wounds were reopened and up went another brick wall.

My knees began to weaken, my hands began to shake, and my tears ran like waterfalls.

The thought I had inside were very crucial, and I was afraid of what may happen next.

Then hurt, pain, and bitterness to over me; and then my heart felt dark and depressed.

I've been through so much hurt throughout my life, and I didn't know what to do.

I should've told you a long time ago, that most of my stress was because of you.

I tried my best to get over you and soon I met someone else.

Which made it even harder to get over you, because he reminded me

so much of yourself.

Emotions

I went from a relationship to just dating and I still ended up alone.

Leaving me feeling abandoned and empty inside, with no man of my own.

It was inside that I cried, it was inside where my heart was broken into two.

It was inside that my soul was taken away, and where I cried for you.

You still don't seem to understand why I feel the way that I do.

Maybe it's because of the betrayal and devastation that I felt you intentionally

put me through.

I've harbored years of agony and frustration all inside of me.

I tried moving forward but couldn't help feeling that a part of me was still missing.

The past is the past and what's done is now done.

The next best thing for me to do is try my best to get over it, and

force myself to move on.

Do you think I'll ever have a chance to have you back in my life?

Emotions

Or end up like you said, "Always a bridesmaid and never someone's wife."

All that I ask of you is if both you and I could sit down and talk.

It's not like I'm asking for a candle lit dinner or romantic midnight walk.

Now what kind of harm do you think will come out of a request such as simple as this?

All I want is your undivided attention. I promise there's no strings attached,

There's no plotting or twists.

You're turning nothing into a little bit of something, for no apparent reason at all.

You're afraid to talk to me, to be around me, or even pick up the phone and call.

All I need is someone there that I know I could talk to.

And I thought maybe or even possibly that someone could be you.

I was left with so many unanswered questions, so many lies and so much exposure.

You didn't even have the common decency or respect to provide me with any closure.

I wasn't going to beg or pressure you into having a conversation with me.

Emotions

The way I was treated during our years of history together will come back on you, you'll see.

Just know that you will reap what you sew when you least expect it. And that karma is so real.

You just lost a good one my friend! Because I'm kind of a big deal.

Don't ever think that I will come back to you or even sit and wait.

For you to grow up and get your life together, because by then it'll be too late.

God doesn't make mistakes. I thought we were meant to be together.

But he showed me that through my pain and brokenness, that he was preparing me for someone better.

Emotions

LET'S STAY TOGETHER

What is this feeling? I can't sleep at night.
The image of you will not leave my sight.
I was wrong, I thought you were "Mr. Right."
Until we started to argue, fuss, and fight.
I thought our relationship would reach new heights.
No one knows the future; either we will, or we might.
Just the thought of it gives me such a fright.
You were my star; you were my shining knight.
I was your jewel that beamed so bright.
Being around you was such a delight.
Now you seem to be so uptight.
Come soar with me on a new journey.
Jump aboard on the next flight.
If we can just start all over, the relationship will be alright.

Emotions

GET TO KNOW ME

Before you judge me, or misinterpret me; understand me first

then try to get to know me.

I always thought "Well maybe it's me." But now I am thinking.

"Well maybe it's him."

Sometimes I think it's best to keep uncertain thoughts within.

There are some things about me that you'll may never comprehend.

All I ask is that you be a little bit more supportive of me and become a better friend.

I know I operate a little differently than most women do.

I would appreciate if you let me be me and focus a lot more on you.

All I ever get from you is sarcasm and negative criticism.

You're never satisfied with what I say or do.

"Will I ever make you happy or will I ever be able to please you?"

Maybe you should start loving me for me and what I stand for.

Emotions

And respect my decisions and beliefs, and everything that I adore.

Whether it be meditating, reading, praying or even writing my poems.

Appreciate me for who I am and try to accept me with open arms.

Please believe me when I say this. I cannot stress it enough.

If you can show me that you can accept me and do a little better at respecting me.

Then you would be a little more easier to love.

Emotions

WHERE DID YOU GO?

When I was all alone, you were there.

When I thought all hope was gone, you were there.

When I needed to be encouraged, you were there.

When I was feeling discouraged, you were there.

When I was weary or sad, you were there.

When I was disappointed or mad, you were there.

When I had no one to turn to, you were there.

When my friends betrayed me, you were there.

When my family played me, you were there.

But now that I need you, you are gone.

Emotions

IT'S GOING TO BE ALRIGHT

Life is not always a bed of roses, nor is it always peaches and cream.

But often time ups, downs, twist, turns, and shattered hopes and dreams.

Don't let the bad things in life get the best of you.

Instead move forward and continue doing what you have to do.

In order to make it, to succeed to move on or to survive.

You have to keep your head up, don't look back but most importantly stay alive.

Things will get better, I promise. It may even take a while.

So bring yourself out of the dumps and turn that frown into a smile.

Soon your hurt, pain, and discomfort will finally come to an end.

I hope you'll always remember these words are encouragement coming from your friend.

SPECIAL BOND

What is this special bond that you and I both share?

It's like I can feel your presence, even when you're not there.

It's a feeling that is so mystical to me.

When you're hurting, I can feel your pain.

Now how can that possible be?

It can be total silence, and I won't hear a sound.

Then I can hear you thinking your thoughts, even though you're not around.

It's so phenomenal that I cannot seem to comprehend.

It's almost like we have that bond, as if you and I were twins.

It's one of those rare coincidences that's somewhat difficult to explain.

At the same time, I'm glad that it's a special bond that we both gained.

Even though we're brother and sister, I hope we'll always remain best friends.

And I hope that this special bond that we share will never be lost or end.

Emotions

MAKE UP YOUR MIND

How can you disrespect me one day, then you're loving towards me the next?

How can you hurt me like that then leave me feeling confused and perplexed?

If you supposedly care about me, why do you treat me this way?

Why do you always leave me, when you know you really want to stay?

How can you play with my emotions knowing how I really feel?

How can you kiss and hug on me like it's really no big deal?

You just can't keep on doing that anytime you please.

Making me think that you want me back, but at the same time being a big tease.

It's about time that you figure out what and who it is that you truly want.

Instead of pretending you don't care about me and acting so nonchalant.

You say one thing but act another way.

You're so unpredictable I can't and at times I just don't understand.

Emotions

Just tell me if you want to be with me, or just remain my friend.

As you can see I don't have the time to play your simple games.

That will certainly drive a person like me totally and completely insane.

So whenever you're ready to settle down and make a commitment to me.

Just le me know we'll give it a try, and hope that we last for eternity.

Emotions

Emotions

I THOUGHT…

What have I done to make you want to hurt me?

What have I said to make you want to desert me?

Is it simply because you just fell out of love?

Or is it because I just wasn't enough?

I thought I was living up to what you expected of me.

I thought I was being the person you wanted me to be.

I thought I was who you wanted to settle down with.

I thought I was the one who showed you everything you missed.

I thought I was your sense of hope, your ray of sunshine.

I thought I'd always be yours, and that you'd always be mine.

Maybe you were just expecting too much of me.

Or trying to make me into something I just couldn't be.

The only thing I knew to do was to be myself.

I guess that wasn't enough for you that's why you left.

I was devastated and had to move on. And I knew it would affect you.

Because you're finally realizing I was the best thing that happened to you.

Emotions

And no one will make you feel the way I do.

I figured it was your loss and someone else's gain.

Because you lost your rainbow that comes at the end of the rain.

But here's the best thing that comes from all of this.

I'm willing to give it another try if that's what you wish.

It's usually one strike with me, and then you're gone.

But I'd give you one more swing, because you're the one I really want.

Maybe this time our relationship can last.

So let's concentrate more on our future, and forget about the past.

This time it's going to work out, I promise. No, I guarantee.

Just as long as you keep your trust and confidence in me.

Emotions

Emotions

SILENCE

Am I moving to fast? Am I moving to slow?

You're not telling me anything, so therefore I don't know.

You're holding things back and keeping things within.

Whatever it is won't change the fact that I will still be your friend.

I can see things coming long before you speak.

But for you to get it out may take days, hours, or often several weeks.

It feels like I'm on a roller coaster, I keep going up and down.

And at times I feel like I'm spinning in a circle, almost as if I'm on a merry-go-round.

I'm glad that you could come to me openly, honestly and sincere.

But deep down inside, I can't explain why I still have that fear.

The fear of loosing the one that I thought was really my "Mr. Right."

Watching you slowly drift into the cold, dark and lonely night.

Emotions

Emotions

ONE DAY AT A TIME

In my heart I know that everything is going to work out for the best.

So please try to forgive me for putting you through all of this stress.

I'll try to be more patient and stop jumping to all these conclusions.

And wait quietly until you come up with a sensible resolution.

You keep on telling me to give you a little more trust.

If that's what I have to do, well then, I guess I must.

I must take things day-by-day and stop trying to figure you out.

Listen when you speak and give you the benefit of the doubt.

We've already explained to one another how each one of us feels.

So, let's leave the situation alone and stop making everything a big deal.

We can try and try until we can't try no more.

Let's wait and see what the future may hold, or what God has for us in store.

I'm willing to wait if that's what you really want to do.

Emotions

That way we'll really know for sure if you're the one for me and I'm the one for you

MISS CARRYING YOU

I'd never thought I'd have a loss such as great as this.

I can still feel you're a part of me and everyday you're deeply missed.

I constantly wonder what we'd be like if you were still in my life.

I can't get the thought of you our o my mind, because I dream about your every single night.

Why would something like this have to happen to someone like me?

Knowing you were the one I always wanted and now knowing you're the one I'll never see.

When you appeared into my life, I know you were sent down from heaven above.

To bring back the happiness in my soul and be that special someone I could forever love.

I'm going to miss your warmth, and your comfort you've shown and given to me.

I'm going to miss your feel and touch, and the way you made me feel free.

But most of all I'm going to miss the loving smile on your face.

Emotions

The one that I dreamed and thought about every night and day.

I know everything in life happens for a reason, and you were definitely no mistake.

If only you could've held on a little bit longer, everything would've turned out great.

I'll never understand what has happened, nor where things unexpectedly went wrong.

It's just saddens me to know that I'll never get to know you,

or have the chance to be your mom.

Emotions

IN LOVE

Oh, what a day, what a wonderful day.

I woke up this morning indulged in your embrace.

The sun is shining through the window, its rays enlighten my soul.

Because I know that I have someone I can love, cherish and hold.

Outside the weather is cool, windy, and bitterly crisp.

My body is then warmed by your soft but sudden kiss.

You set off a spark that made me feel rather tingly inside.

And knowing that you are a part of my life, gives me so much security and pride.

I feel so lucky, better yet I feel so blessed.

It's an emotion that's unexplanatory so don't try to guess.

Just continue on doing what it is that you do.

To keep me falling in deeper love with you.

Emotions

I'M HERE FOR YOU

You opened your eyes today baby, it's one thing I knew you'd soon achieve.

I was able to see you, but were you able to see me?

You don't know how happy that made me to see you open your eyes.

It overwhelmed me so much that all I could do was cry.

The emotions that had taken over me, was just so hard to explain.

But don't worry I was comforted and consoled by your family and friends.

I know your recovery will take some time, but oh what progress you've shown.

I will be here for better or for worse, so don't ever think that I'd leave you alone.

You've come too far to turn back now, and I thank God for pulling you through.

I will take care of you as long as time permits because that's what friends do.

Emotions

CHOSEN

When I first laid eyes on you, I know that you were the one.

The one that I had prayed and asked God for, the beginning of my life has now begun.

It appears as if my life has been remotely rewound.

It seems as if my frowns have turned up-side down.

I no longer have to experience loneliness nor feel restricted or bound.

I didn't have to find you; you chose me and now I've been found.

A man that findeth a wife is said to have found a good thing.

Not only did you find the right woman, but you have also found your blessing.

What God has put together, let no man put asunder.

I'll be your bolt of lightning and you'll be my thunder.

Which such strong forces nothing can pull us apart.

Because the love that we have for each other is so strong in our hearts.

Emotions

MY TRUE LOVE

There's this smile on my face that I cannot explain.

There's some joy in my heart; I no longer feel that pain.

There are more giggles when I laugh, almost as if I were a child.

I haven't felt this way in a very long while.

What is this feeling that's so hard for me to explain?

Where did all this love come from that I suddenly gained?

What are all these emotions stirring up inside of my soul?

Could it be love? Oh, how I wish someone would let me know.

Maybe that someone could be you.

Maybe you're the one who has made me feel brand new.

Maybe you're the one that God sent from above.

Maybe you're the one whose been showing me how to love.

Maybe I'm getting too excited thinking about all of this.

I guess I'm making up for all the years that I've missed.

Of the energy, excitement and happiness.

Of the love, joy, and state of bliss.

All of this shows me how God is real.

Emotions

He picked me up, turned me around, an brought me out of my lonely ordeal.

All of this also shows me how the word of God is true.

Because he answered my prayers by sending me you.

Ask and you shall receive, knock and the door shall open.

He's granted all my wishes and responded to every work I've spoken.

So, I thank you Lord for sending me this man, and for allowing me to experience love again.

LOOK TO GOD

Life is too short, and it is what you make it.

Tomorrow isn't promised, so take hold of your situation and overtake it.

Just know in your situation of test and trials, you are going to go through.

God said it was supposed to happen, so now what are you going to do?

Sit there and complain, become depressed, and just cry?

You need to lift your head up and wipe those tears from your eyes.

We serve a God that's bigger than our problems, and that's so much stronger.

All those hurts, pains, and disappointments; you shall have no longer.

Just stay focused and be encouraged, because God will see you through.

And always know that He loves you and has his angels watching over you.

LET'S MAKE IT WORK

If I had a penny for your thoughts. If I could only gaze into your mind.

I would soon have the answer to why you decided to leave me behind.

If I had to sacrifice my time to make things between us right.

I'd do anything to save this relationship and remain by your side.

Can you please just give me one more chance to love you?

Can you picture being with me the rest of your life?

Can you give me one more chance to show you, that I'm willing to give

us one more try.

We belong together baby, I know we were meant to be.

I hope we can last forever. No more interference or distractions.

It will just be you and me.

Because baby I love you, I need you, I want you.

And I know that you feel the same way too.

What is it about you that all the ladies love so much?

Emotions

Why is it that when they talk to you, they feel the need to touch?

It's an uncontrollable desire they have that they can't keep under submission.

When they come talk to you it's almost as if I would like for them to ask my permission.

The sight of it bothers me so much I can't even explain.

Just the thought of it sickens me, I can no longer sustain.

I never thought that I'd ever become this annoyed or overly jealous.

You've explained to them our situation, but their actions are somewhat rebellious.

"Try to ignore it." You say. Well, I don't know if I can.

Because I can't completely get over the fact that all these women

want my man.

It's no "Big Deal", as you so called put.

I guess you'd understand a little more about how I feel,

if the show was on the other foot.

I've tried not to say anything, but now I feel confined.

Hopefully all of this will change later in time.

Please help me by sparing me the embarrassment.

Emotions

And let me let these women know there's no need for the physical

contact or harassment.

So do whatever it is that you feel you must.

In order for me to feel secure or to have any trust.

I don't know if this was something I failed to mention.

I will walk away, because there's no need for me to feel

that there is any competition.

It's not that I don't love you, or that I don't care.

But one thing you need to understand, is that I'm not willing to share.

Figure what's important to you and decide if you want me to stay.

Put your foot down, make sure you put these disrespectful women in their place.

Emotions

A PART OF YOU

If it weren't for you, I wouldn't be here today.

Just a figment of your imagination, or a molecule in space.

I give you the thanks for showing such a miraculous deed.

In creating my life by sparing your seed.

You showed your true intentions by always being there.

You showed true love, stepped up, and showed how much you cared.

A lot of men wouldn't want the extra responsibility.

But you showed up and you did it willingly.

No one had to nag you, manipulate you or beg.

You gave it your all, and gave all that you had.

Your time and affection, your love and attention.

A shoulder to cry on along with many great things to mention.

The sound of your voice and the warmth from your touch.

Anything besides that, I don't remember that much.

I remember mommy being so relaxed and content,

as I lay there inside awaiting the moment.

To meet you and greet you, and to see your big smile.

These 9 months seemed like a very long while.

Emotions

The suspense of wondering if I'd be your son or your daughter.

All I know now is that,

God couldn't have blessed me with a better father.

About Juanita

Juanita Edwards: A Life of Faith, Family, and Purpose

Juanita Edwards, born in Washington, DC, and now residing in Ohio, is a devoted wife of 24 years, proud mother of six children (four biological), grandmother (affectionately known as Gigi) of five, and godmother to five beautiful young ladies.

As the second youngest of five siblings, Juanita spent her childhood traveling the world due to her father's military career. This upbringing nurtured her love for exploring and appreciating the beauty of God's creation. Her father instilled in her the belief that the world is full of wonders waiting to be discovered, a lesson she cherishes to this day.

For the past 26 years, Juanita has been a self-employed entrepreneur, owning and directing multiple childcare facilities in Ohio and teaching preschool. Her passion lies in working with children of all ages and abilities, advocating for their right to be loved and educated regardless of challenges. This mission stems from the example set by her mother, Brenda J. Lambert, whose nurturing spirit and unwavering love inspired Juanita's dedication to caregiving.

Juanita's late parents, Brenda J. Lambert and Darryl G. Lambert, also fostered her entrepreneurial spirit and love for creative pursuits like skating and writing poetry. Their legacy lives on in her commitment to family, creativity, and purposeful living.

In addition to her professional endeavors, Juanita mentors and coaches young mothers, providing resources and guidance to help them navigate life's challenges. Her personal motto, "If I got it, you got it," reflects her deep desire to uplift others and share the blessings she has received.

In her leisure time, Juanita enjoys traveling, roller skating, writing poetry, and cherishing moments with her family. Her writing serves as a vessel to motivate, inspire, and heal, with the ultimate goal of encouraging others to thrive.

Above all, Juanita attributes her journey and accomplishments to her faith in Yahweh, whom she credits for shaping her into the woman she is today. Her unwavering trust in Him has molded her into a loving wife, mother, grandmother, entrepreneur, and role model.

With gratitude for her life's blessings, Juanita eagerly embraces the next chapter, ready to share her story and inspire others to overcome obstacles, walk in their purpose, and shine brightly.

Emotions

www.ingramcontent.com/pod-product-compliance
Lightning Source LLC
Chambersburg PA
CBHW051931160426
43198CB00012B/2104